LOVE & RESPECT

AF491507

The Respect He Desperately Needs

The concept of love in language
Love in language is defined as a great and strong feeling that one feels in the direction of someone, which makes him attracted to him emotionally strongly and influenced by him, he wants to share all the moments of his life and stay with him forever, a beautiful feeling in which one sees one's partner very important to him and makes it one of his priorities, and synonyms many deep terms, such as love, and pride in the beloved

The Love She Most Desires

The Love She Most Desires

One is puzzled when one notices a change in his feelings towards his partner, and may hesitate to reveal or acknowledge them until they are verified, and understand their cause and nature, but love is a clear feeling and a strong emotion that is difficult to keep secret and hide as mentioned before, and therefore must show its clear signs on its owner, including the following:[7]

•••
’’

•••••••••
’’’’’’’’

Love

Love is defined as a
set of complex feelings
that result in many
actions and ideas
woven with strong
emotions that govern
and control one's being
and sense, making him
want to protect the
person or the thing he
loves, and feel with

affection, familiarity and great kindness towards him, respect him and preserve him and take into account his feelings and want to delight and protect him from any threat or danger that may harm him in any way,   It is not limited to

human love for each
other only, one may
love a pet and give him
care, care and
compassion and seek
to protect and preserve
it, or be associated
with a special inner
feeling such as
freedom,
independence, entity

and personality, or
self-love for example

. . . .

. . . .

. . . .

. . . . What is love?
*Love in language is
defined as a great and
strong feeling that one
feels in the direction of*

someone, which makes him attracted to him emotionally strongly and influenced by it, he wants to share all the moments of his life and stay with him forever, a beautiful feeling in which one sees one's partner very important to him and makes it one of his priorities, and synonyms many deep terms, such as love, pride in the beloved, a strong desire to take care of him and take care of him constantly, a feeling that grows and increases over time, in which the lover likes his lover and becomes a source of inspiration and passion and cause One of the reasons for happiness and comfort

The concept of love in psychology

Although psychologists lack the ability and accuracy of the poets, they have also worked hard to

express and
define the
feeling of love
through
scientific
research and
biological and

practical
experiments on
the people
under its
influence, some
of whom have
identified and

summarized factors that result in this feeling in one principle: communication, participation

and support,
which results in
a very
interconnected
and strong
relationship
between the

parties,
resulting in
great emotional
and
physiological
feelings
centered

around care,
protection,
attention,
kindness,
excitement and
other feelings
that may

similar to what was mentioned earlier about this deep passion

Philosophers'
definition of
love differs
from other
concepts of
poets and
scholars, where

their concepts
varied, and
some
considered it
merely a word
that does not
express

anything
concrete and
reasonable or
linked to a clear
truth, while
others see it as
a strong

influence and a great means of controlling the entity and the world in retrospect once it falls under its

influence,
others
preferred not to
interpret it and
leave it in a
world far from
curiosity,

application and research, but despite their different interpretation and definitions can not deny the fact that this feeling is fundamental and important, and has a great role And a tangible impact

on people of
different
cultures and
races, so they
continued to
develop
philosophical

theories and interpretations to try to reach a clear definition and a fixed concept of it, but according

to their
opinions these
theories varied
and conflicted
and varied with
the progress of
life and the

maturity of
human beings
and different
needs and way
of thinking

Scientists have had many questions about why one feels love, some of them considered it a complex thing that needs a lot of research and study, as the nature of this feeling and its amount and

effect varies
from person to
person, love
may begin with
a look and a
simple meeting
in which one

has a feeling of attraction to the other party, but it grows and develops over time to become an urgent goal

to get closer to
it more,
divided by
some
researchers for
stages
according to its

depth and the
effect of human
hormones on its
owner, as it
may be a
common need
to satisfy the

innate desire
for them, and
as a reason for
the
development
and
reproduction of

races over time, through mating between different factions to sustain the human race,

and in other
cases love is a
distinct
phenomenon
that makes
people attract
to each other

under the
influence of
different
hormones such
as dopamine
released by the
brain, which in

turn makes one more attached to one's partner, increases his enthusiasm, excitement,

activity, and
sense

With the
vitality that
may lose the
ability to sleep
due to the
frequent
thinking of the

partner, it shows signs of tension, low appetite, insomnia, and sometimes discomfort, and

it may develop
in some to
become a sense
of love and
madness that
accompanies
the situations of

attraction and intense attachment to this person and the frequent thinking of him, while this

love may reach
the stage of
association,
which is one of
the static stages
resulting from
stable long-

term relationships in which the parties share feelings and go beyond the earlier stages

and reach a
feeling of
completeness
and happiness
with the
presence of the
party The other

in their lives
they keep it in,
and they work
hard to support
tlationship and
make it stable,
healthy and

successful

One is confused, when one notices a change in his feelings towards his partner, and

may hesitate to
reveal or
recognize them
until they are
verified, and
understand
their cause and

nature, but love is a clear feeling and a strong emotion that is difficult to hide and hide as mentioned before, and therefore must show its clear signs on its owner, some of which come

The inner signs
of love are the
feelings and
feelings that
one has, deep,
and sincere,
which one has

for one's lover, most notably the following: [7] the tendency to amplify the positive qualities of the partner, to see him as a complete and distinguished person, and to overlook some of his negatives

and mistakes
motivated by
great affection
towards him,
and therefore
the lover looks
at him as

different and
prominent from
all around him,
and

exaggerates his
feeling without
thinking of

anything else
even though he
may be a
normal person.
Feeling cheerful
and happy for
the beloved, if

he succeeds or
accomplishes
one of his goals,
and not to feel
inferiority,
jealousy or
inferiority

towards him,
but quite the
contrary to
support him
and pride in
him and
congratulate

him and feel
sincere and true
happiness and
good wishes for
him. Influenced
by the opinions
of the beloved

strongly and comply with his ideas and attention to them, as one may be accustomed to

making his
personal
decisions in
particular and
individually,
but the
presence of a

lover in his life
feels his
direction of
affection and
familiarity may
make him want
to share the

planning and care for his ideas and opinions and influence them, which may conflict with his

desires
sometimes but
his great love
will push him
to compromise
for the
happiness and

satisfaction of
his lover

There are some spontaneous and gentle physical signs in which one tries to express one's sincere feelings towards the beloved, through the language of the body, including: [8] a sincere and spontaneous smile: a smile expresses happiness and good mood, and one often

smiles in the
face of the
person who is
happy, so his
constant
attractive smile
in the face of

those who love
is proof of his
desire to stay
with him and
communicate
more, and a
sense of joy and

comfort. Visual communication : The positive visual response of focusing on the eyes of the other party,

and looking at
them at length
directly, is
evidence of
interest in it,
while the shift
away from it

and the
inability to
communicate
visually
indicate a lack
of interest, or
sometimes

deception, so constant eye glances and focus are on the things a person loves and is attracted to.

Philosophers consider that the word love is not linked to a realistic or real order, but love since the time of the ancient Greeks was a pillar of basic philosophy, as many philosophical theories emerged that consider love a physical phenomenon that expresses the animal genetic desire

for human
behavior, and
other theories
have stipulated
that love is a
spiritual
material that

elevates human beings and elevates them to the level of divinity, as the philosopher Aristotle

described love
as two bodies
and a spirit
One. [1] Love
can be defined
as a strong
admiration

feeling that a
person feels
towards a
friend or
relative or the
direction of
something, and

the most
common
definition of
love is the
feeling of
admiring
another adult,

and being romantically attracted to it. [2] All historical facts that sought to justify and

interpret love
are totally
inadequate,
because all the
characteristics
of love can be
interpreted and

translated by science, but love itself cannot be explained, and some characteristics of love are not shared and mutual among all lovers, as the personal nature of love is different. [3]

Several studies were conducted on love and how it occurs, including one conducted by a research team led by scientist Helen Fisher in 2005, which made images using functional MRI technology for the brains of a group of university students, as scientists allowed these students to see

and
photograph
their university
colleagues
using
functional MRI
technology, and

then reimagine
them again
after seeing
pictures of
someone they
love, and this
process was

performed on nearly 2,500 students, noted

In the images, when the student sees the person he

loves, his brain
has become
more active in
dopamine-rich
areas, also
called the
neurotransmitt

er responsible for good sensation r, and two areas of the brain have shown activity in functional

MRI scans, the
guilt core area,
an area
associated with
the discovery
and prediction
of rewards and

the integration
of sensory
experiences
with the social
behavior of the
individual, the
ventricular

ceiling area, an area associated with pleasure and focused attention, and incentives to help get

rewards. [4]

The concept of love has been defined in many forms and types throughout ancient philosophical history, where the types of love are distinguished from each other by different

forms of desires
and emotions
that accompany
each form, and
with different
types of love, it
is natural that

some types of
love are good
for the person
and his health,
and others may
be harmful to
him, and it is

worth noting
that Western
culture is based
on four main
types of love
that were taken
from the

ancient Greek culture and each type was named In a certain Greek word,[6][7] these species can be mentioned as follows: [6]

The meaning of love can be defined from several points of view as follows: [1] Love holds the

point of view of
romance as
perfection, so
that it is
believed that
both parties
should

understand
each other and
have no
differences at
all, although
the existence of
such an idea

may seem a
form of
imagination
and idealism
that may make
the relationship
unhealthy.

Love holds the point of view of science in the sense of smell, as love represents a human sense of

smell through
the idea of
attracting a
particular
person, where
scientists
believe that

there are
complex genes
in the dna
tissue that
drive a person
to feel his love
for someone

else. Love holds a real person's point of view in the sense that it resembles an ocean, where love carries a

lot of changes
over time, it is
just like the
ocean
potentially
having
permanent

ripples such as tides, and this view may be considered the most rational and realistic, meaning that

love is not easy
at all and may
even need
effort and hard
work in order
to .

www.ingramcontent.com/pod-product-compliance
Lightning Source LLC
Chambersburg PA
CBHW081344160726
48000CB00010B/3224